A Catholic Woman's Book of Prayers

DONNA-MARIE COOPER O'BOYLE

PARACLETE PRESS
BREWSTER, MASSACHUSETTS

2017 First printing this edition

A Catholic Woman's Book of Prayers

Copyright © 2017 by Donna-Marie Cooper O'Boyle

Original edition copyright © 2010 by Donna-Marie Cooper O'Boyle. Published by Our Sunday Visitor, Inc., Huntington, IN.

The Scripture citations used in this work are taken from the *Catholic Edition of the Revised Standard Version of the Bible* (RSV), copyright © 1965 and 1966 by the Division of Christian Education of the National Council of the Churches of Christ in the United States of America. Used by permission. All rights reserved.

English translations of Vatican documents are courtesy of the Vatican website, www.vatican.va.

English translation of the *Catechism of the Catholic Church* for the United States of America, copyright © 1994, United States Catholic Conference, Inc.—Libreria Editrice Vaticana. English translation of the *Catechism of the Catholic Church: Modifications from the Editio Typica*, copyright © 1997, United States Catholic Conference, Inc.—Libreria Editrice Vaticana.

The Paraclete Press name and logo (dove on cross) are trademarks of Paraclete Press, Inc.

Library of Congress Cataloging-in-Publication Data
Names: O'Boyle, Donna-Marie Cooper, author.
Title: A Catholic woman's book of prayers / Donna-Marie Cooper O'Boyle.
Description: Brewster MA : Paraclete Press Inc., 2017. | Originally
    published: Huntington, Ind. : Our Sunday Visitor Pub., 2010.
Identifiers: LCCN 2017008678 | ISBN 9781612619217 (trade pbk.)
Subjects: LCSH: Catholic women--Prayers and devotions.
Classification: LCC BX2170.W7 O26 2017 | DDC 242/.802--dc23
LC record available at https://lccn.loc.gov/2017008678

10 9 8 7 6 5 4 3 2 1

Published by Paraclete Press
Brewster, Massachusetts
www.paracletepress.com
Printed in the United States of America

CONTENTS

• • • • • • • • •

Dedicated with all my love to all my children:
Justin, Chaldea, Jessica, Joseph, and Mary-Catherine
And to my grandson, Shepherd James

• • • • • • • • •

It is truly an awe-inspiring gift to be a woman. We are blessed indeed. But sometimes, due to life's arduous challenges and this darkened culture's crazy mixed messages, or simply from a lack of awareness of our God-given gifts, we women can feel totally worn down and insignificant. But women are magnificent—strong and heroic! We are endowed with immeasurable God-given gifts. We possess exquisite dignity, and with God's grace, we have the ability and power to make a huge difference in our world.

Look at St. Teresa of Calcutta. I was blessed to know her for about ten years, and I'll never forget when I met her. She was so tiny—not much taller than my young daughter at the time—and she looked awfully frail. But she was a powerhouse of faith, hope, and love! And full of spunk, too! She showed us that love often requires sacrifice to be authentic, and that another kind of hunger exists in our world, a hunger for love. Many people around us are among the walking wounded, starving for love, affirmation, and encouragement.

Let's pray to emulate Mother Teresa's virtues and strive to reach beyond our comfort zones to offer Christ's love to others. And, let us never forget, Mother Teresa was a woman—the supposed "weaker" sex. Her "yes" to God, not once, but twice, encourages us to do the same—to respond to his holy will in our life with our own unique and wholehearted "yes."

I love what Archbishop Fulton Sheen expressed about women:

> Which stands up better in a crisis—man or woman? The best way to arrive at a conclusion is to go to the greatest crisis the world ever faced, namely, the Crucifixion of our Divine Lord. When we come to this great drama of Calvary there is one fact that stands out very clearly: *men failed*. . . . On the other hand, there is not a single instance of a woman's failing Jesus.[1]

Women have huge hearts. There is no doubt about it. God blesses women with the gift to *be there* for others, to *remain* beside them during their pain and struggles, to *offer* love and prayers.

St. John Paul II in 1988 praised women for their gifts and their dignity in his Apostolic Letter *Mulieris Dignitatem: On the Dignity and Vocation of Women*, and again in 1995 in his *Letter to Women*. Writing at length, he concluded with these words:

> Thank you, *every woman*, for the simple fact of being *a woman*! Through the insight which is so much a part of your womanhood you enrich the world's understanding and help to make human relations more honest and authentic.[2]

St. John Paul II also reminded us:

> The moral and spiritual strength of a woman is joined to her awareness that God entrusts the human being to her in a special way.
>
> Of course, God entrusts every human being to each and every other human being. But this entrusting concerns women in a special way—precisely by reason of their femininity—and this in a particular way determines their vocation.[3]

These words give today's women much to ponder: All women are entrusted with all human beings! This is indeed a high calling.

Women have been blessed with an innate femininity born in hearts that are meant to be generous—hearts that can help to heal wounds, bridge gaps, and soothe the suffering and demanding. Let us pray that all women will discover their true God-given femininity. In addition, let us pray and ponder our own part in this ongoing journey of helping others with Christ's love.

As you read through this book, take time to pray for a deeper awareness of the "entrusting" of which St. John Paul II spoke, so that all your encounters can blossom into a healing balm for those near you—particularly women and girls who may be struggling to make sense of their roles and the multiplicity of challenges that beset them, the unreasonable demands for perfection placed on them, and the countless other contradictions aimed at them by our culture. Women everywhere can benefit from prayers, encouragement, concern, and love. You can be a beautiful vessel of God's grace to other women.

I encourage you to take this book with you to Adoration of Jesus in the Blessed Sacrament, where you can pray and ponder deeply while with Our Eucharistic Lord. And use it wherever you may be throughout your busy days. May this book be a holy boost to your spirits as you strive to get closer and closer to Jesus. May God bless your journey as you extend your hand and heart to those on your path!

CHAPTER ONE

Every Woman— A Unique Gift

This word of thanks to the Lord for his mysterious plan regarding the vocation and mission of women in the world is at the same time a concrete and direct word of thanks to women, to every woman, for all that they represent in the life of humanity.

—St. John Paul II, *Letter to Women*

BEING A WOMAN

Women fill numerous roles in a variety of vocations. Each woman is exceptionally unique and irreplaceable, possessing her own personal gifts to offer the world. Our Lord Jesus is said to have told St. Gertrude the Great, "My heaven would not be complete without you." We are reminded that every woman is a dear daughter of God. These are beautiful, affirming words for women to ponder in their hearts.

Help Me to Discover My Gifts, Lord

Dear Lord, open my eyes to discover my gifts as a woman.
Open my heart to feel Your loving embrace of me as Your daughter,
    affirming my dignity in Your eyes;
Open my arms wide so they will stretch outward to others, loving and
    serving them with Your love, Lord.
Help me never to lose sight of who I am and who You created me to be.
Thank You for the glorious gift of being a woman!

THE SINGLE WOMAN

A single woman can be single for a time or single forever, depending upon her state of life. A woman is single until she enters matrimony or religious life—or may remain single her entire life, not being called to the Sacrament of Marriage or to be a nun. The single state of life is a vocation, too. Certainly, single women are busy with their various duties. However, the single vocation may afford a woman the time to minister to others, since she does not have the responsibility of a spouse or children.

Show Me, Lord

Please Lord, help me to recognize where there is a need to lend a hand, where there is a hunger for love that my smile or gentle touch can satiate.

Help me not to succumb to the temptations of the culture, which dictate a way of life that contradicts my faith. Show me how to navigate my single life in the way that pleases You most.

> *But they who wait for the LORD shall renew their strength, they shall mount up with wings like eagles, they shall run and not be weary, they shall walk and not faint.*
> *—Isaiah 40:31*

Blessed Mother Mary, please mother me as I tread through each day, striving to come closer to your Son, Jesus, amid the temptations, allurements, and contradictions of our world. Amen.

THE MARRIED WOMAN

The gift of the Sacrament of Marriage may cause a wife to experience the heights of incredible joy and bubble over with sentimental emotion at times. Perhaps there also will be times when she wonders how she can live even one more day in the same household with her "dear husband" who is driving her crazy! During the challenging times, it is wise to do our best to smile and recall that our role as a Catholic wife is to help get our husband to heaven—with God's amazing grace! With the greatest of joys and most arduous of challenges, marriage is a blessed and powerful partnership in which you love, serve, and do everything possible to draw your spouse closer to God. Don't forget to call upon the graces of the Sacrament of Marriage when praying for your husband. Those graces are powerful!

. . . .

Holy Scripture affirms that man and woman were created for one
another: "It is not good that the man should be alone."
The woman, "flesh of his flesh," his equal, his nearest in all
things, is given to him by God as a "helpmate"; she thus
represents God from whom comes our help.
—CCC, 1605

. . . .

Dear Blessed Mother Mary, you loved your husband, St. Joseph, with an exceptional love. Help me to offer my love to my husband unreservedly throughout the give and take of daily life and always to keep his eternal salvation in mind and in my prayers. Amen.

· ·

Marriage is an act of will that signifies and involves a mutual gift, which unites the spouses and binds them to their eventual souls, with whom they make up a sole family—a domestic church.
—St. John Paul II

· ·

Praying Through Bliss and Clashing

Dear Lord, thank You for blessing me with the vocation of marriage in which I am privileged to experience the sanctified union of two souls. If I dared meditate deeply upon this aspect alone, I would realize how noble my vocation actually is: a means of sanctification for one another. Guide me each day, dear Lord, through all the joys and those tough spots, too, to surrender my will to You so that I will be the wife You want me to be—one who loves with Your love and who desires to help open the gates of heaven for my husband through my selfless love for his soul.

THE VOCATION OF MOTHERHOOD

To be bestowed with the vocation of motherhood, whether biologically or through adoption, is to be blessed straight down to the core of our being. What other vocation cooperates with God and one's spouse to accept the gift of life? Motherhood is a tremendous calling, the responsibility of raising little saints to heaven! An amazing amount of sanctification goes on throughout a mother's demanding days within her domestic church—so many grace-filled moments exist within the "little things" of mothering. Saints are made right at home by means of the love of a faithful and prayerful mother!

COMMUNION WITH THE MYSTERY OF LIFE

* *

Motherhood involves a special communion with the mystery of life, as it develops in the mother's womb. The mother is filled with wonder at this mystery of life, and understands with unique intuition what is happening inside her. From the beginning the mother accepts and loves the child she is carrying in her womb.

—St. John Paul II

* *

Dear Mother Mary, teach me your loving motherly ways
so that I may learn to love like you. Amen.

St. Frances of Rome said:

> It is most laudable in a married woman to be devout,
> but she must never forget that she is a housewife and
> sometimes must leave God at the altar to find Him in
> her housekeeping.

A mother can discover God within the nitty-gritty tasks she
lovingly performs in her home. She need only peer into the
eyes of family members she serves to find Jesus there. While
she may desire to be at Adoration or Mass more frequently,
she need not worry that she is missing out on time with Jesus,
since she is serving Him in each of the members of her family.
Rest assured, dear mother, that Our Lord understands your
heart and appreciates that you are serving Him devotedly in
your family.

Bless My Unborn Baby, Lord

As my child grows within me, nourished by my life and love, please
bless me with the extraordinary graces of motherhood and help my baby
flourish with life so that he or she may grow to serve You. Amen.

Guide Me to Guide My Children

Oh, dear Lord, thank You for the gift of motherhood! Help me to guide my children to know the truth of our Faith and lead them closer and closer to You each day. Please bless me with all the graces I need to mother them well. Amen.

• •

Thank you, women who are mothers! You have sheltered human beings within yourselves in a unique experience of joy and travail. This experience makes you become God's own smile upon the newborn child, the one who guides your child's first steps, who helps it to grow, and who is the anchor as the child makes its way along the journey of life.
—St. John Paul II

• •

SINGLE MOTHERS

I was once a single mother. A mother generally doesn't plan to become single during her journey; having a spouse as a partner and best friend is indeed a great help in parenting children, and a dependable, loving support for her as well. There are many single mothers. Some have lost their spouse due to his passing, while many more are missing that other half because of the awful agony of divorce. Although our

Church does not promote divorce, at times, due to assorted grave problems, divorce is the only remedy for a family to live safely and in peace. Therefore, we should never judge divorced women who are striving to do their very best in their circumstances. Rather, we should extend our hand to help them whenever we are able.

Dear Blessed Mother Mary, you were once a single mother. You understand the responsibilities and heartaches as well as the joys. Please intercede for me as I mother my children. Amen.

Help Me, Lord

Lord, my heart feels pierced through at times because I have been left with the responsibility of raising my family alone.

Heal the wounds in my heart, please, Lord.

Help me to forgive those I need to forgive. Give me the strength I need to put one foot in front of the other each day to walk in faith, serving and loving my family and guiding them to You.

DISCOVERING JOY AMID HARDSHIP

When I was a single mother experiencing tough times financially, my birthday came with Christmas fast approaching. My children gave me sweet little handmade gifts and baked a cake, and our lovely celebration warmed my heart. Later that evening, I found an envelope on my bureau with "Mom" written across it. I opened it and, to my astonishment, found one hundred dollars in small bills and a little note: "Dear Mom, Maybe this could help you buy Christmas presents. Love, Chaldea." My teenage daughter had given me all the money she had earned babysitting so that I could buy Christmas gifts. She wanted no credit for herself. Her gift of love pierced my heart.

Incredible joy abounds even during the tough times. Look for it—it is undeniably present!

I love You, Jesus! Open my eyes and my heart to Your love and joy.

consecrated women

The authenticity of a consecrated Sister's commitment is expressed each day as she lives her blessed vows, betrothed to the Lord, and makes her way to heaven—leading others, too, one prayer and act of loving service at a time.

* *

Thank you, consecrated women! Following the example of the greatest of women, the Mother of Jesus Christ, the Incarnate Word, you open yourselves with obedience and fidelity to the gift of God's

love. You help the Church and all mankind to experience a "spousal" relationship to God, one which magnificently expresses the fellowship which God wishes to establish with his creatures.
—St. John Paul II, *Mulieris Dignitatem*

. . . .

Spouse of Jesus

Dear Lord, You have blessed me with a unique union with Yourself. Please grant me the graces I most need in living out my vows to You wholeheartedly and with intense love. Help me to see You within each person I serve—whether in the convent or outside its doors. Pleasing You is my heart's desire.

. . . .

To be a woman means to love and to suffer. To be a nun means to love and suffer more. To be a nun means to enlarge one's capacity for being a woman.
—St. Teresa of Ávila

. . . .

Guide me, Lord. Bless me, please. I love You, Lord!

. . . .

It's your obligation to speak the truth, and everyone can either take it or leave it. But truth must be in us. We live in such poverty of the truth today.
—Mother Angelica

. . . .

Purity is not merely the absence of sensuality; it is selflessness
born of love and the highest love of all.
—Archbishop Fulton Sheen

. . . .

May Your name forever remain on my lips: Jesus, Jesus, Jesus!

. . . .

Take God for your spouse and friend and walk with Him
continually, and you will not sin, will learn to love, and the
things you must do will work out prosperously for you.
—St. Teresa of Ávila

. . . .

SPIRITUAL MOTHERHOOD

Mother Mary is a spiritual mother to us. Spiritual motherhood is a beautiful vocation woven within a woman's vocation to holiness. Women who are not biological or adoptive mothers can act as a spiritual mother to many. They can also pray for certain people—be their "mother." Nuns and sisters and other spiritual mothers of souls imitate the Blessed Mother. St. Teresa Benedicta said:

Woman naturally seeks to embrace that which is living, personal, and whole. To cherish, guard and protect, nourish, and advance growth is her natural, maternal yearning. . . . That is why total surrender which is the principle of the religious life is simultaneously the only adequate fulfillment possible for woman's yearning.

* *

For whoever does the will of my Father in heaven
is my brother, and sister, and mother.
—Matthew 12:50

* *

Blessed Mother Mary, please be a Mother to me and show me how to spiritually mother others.

* *

In three different ways, woman can fulfill the mission of motherliness: in marriage, in the practice of a profession that values human development, and under the veil as the spouse of Christ.
— St. Teresa Benedicta of the Cross (Edith Stein)

* *

St. Teresa Benedicta said:

Everywhere the need exists for maternal sympathy and help, and thus we are able to recapitulate in the one word motherliness that which we have developed as the characteristic value of woman. Only, the motherliness must be that which does not remain within the narrow circle of blood relations or of personal friends; but in accordance with the model of the Mother of Mercy, it must have its root in universal divine love for all who are there, belabored and burdened.

St. Teresa of Calcutta gave us a practical and vital way to view our giving: "We should learn how to give. But we should not regard giving as an obligation, but as a desire."

Dear Jesus, please plant deeply in my heart a heaping dose of faith, hope, and love, so that I may be able to pass it on to all those who are encircled by my motherly care. Deepen my desire to give. Amen.

A REFLECTION ON A WOMAN'S VOCATION

Take some time to meditate on your vocation as a woman. While at times our world may cause you to feel inadequate or unimportant—or seem to imply that you are *just* a woman—you must strive to recognize deep in your heart that Our Lord has blessed you with amazing gifts as a woman. Through prayer and God's grace, you will feel a deep peace in your heart because He loves you so.

CHAPTER TWO

The Joys of Womanhood

Thou hast put more joy in my heart
than they have when their
grain and wine abound.

—Psalm 4:7

St. John Bosco, known for playing games with poor and delinquent boys, told this story:

> A saint was once asked, while playing happily with his companions, what he would do if an angel told him that in a quarter of an hour he would die and have to appear before the judgment seat of God. The saint promptly replied that he would continue playing, because "I am certain these games are pleasing to God."

Let's remember these words the next time we feel a bit guilty for partaking in some fun or taking time out to play with our children. Yes, we work hard at our salvation and in all our duties—but we have to make some room to play as well. I recommend that you carve out time soon to be playful!

. . . .

Joy is a net in which to catch souls.
—St. Teresa of Calcutta

. . . .

DON'T SAVE THE GOOD CHINA!

One day when my mother was lying in her hospital bed ill with cancer, she decided that life was much too short to save the good china for special occasions. She vowed that when she got home, she would start using her fancy dishes stored away in her china cabinet. Sadly, my mother never made it home from the hospital to use her china, but we can all learn from her. Let's use our good china with joy. And make sure to have regular family dinners, too; they certainly show your love for your family. Most importantly, strive to make every day a celebration of life. Having a joyful heart is contagious and will help all those around us, too.

THE DIGNITY OF BEING A WOMAN

If women only knew the magnificent dignity they possess in Our Lord's eyes, they would be bursting with joy at every moment. This awareness alone would be enough to sustain them, come what may.

Our world can be very cold and heartless, and sadly, women can lose the awareness of their God-given dignity along the way. Additionally, with so many tasks on their to-do lists, they can't find the time to stop and ponder their beautiful dignity as women. So pray to unearth your God-given dignity and offer your heart to others in a gesture of joy!

• •

For you shall go out in joy, and be led forth in peace; the mountains and the hills before you shall break forth into singing, and all the trees of the field shall clap their hands.

—Isaiah 55:12

• •

Help Me, Lord

Dear Lord, thank You for the incredible gift of dignity You have blessed me with as a daughter of God! Please increase my awareness of this awesome gift with each passing day. Help me to extend my hands and my heart to others in a welcome expression of love and joy. Amen.

Dear Mother Mary, please guide me ever closer to your Son, Jesus, so that all my prayers and actions will radiate His joy to others. Amen.

GOD-GIVEN GIFTS

As Mother Teresa said, in a letter to me:

> God has given you many gifts; make sure you use them for the glory of God and the good of the people. You have been created to be holy.

Among the gifts we women possess are receptivity (which is at the foundation of all of our feminine gifts), sensitivity (which is not weakness, but indeed a wonderful strength), generosity (available to welcome life and to give), and maternity (biological and spiritual).Women possess warm and loving hearts that reach out to those in need, intuition and insight to help discern where there are wrongs that need correcting, perseverance, patience, compassion, gentleness, sensitivity, and tenderness. Women are great caregivers; they have nurturing spirits, deep inner strength, and determination and passion. God has gifted women with big hearts to bring God's love to others. Let's take some time to think about using our God-given gifts.

Dear Lord, please help me to discover my gifts and use them for Your glory. And help me to assist other women in discovering their own unique gifts. Amen.

* *

We have been created to love and be loved.
—St. Teresa of Calcutta

* *

A WOMAN'S GIFTS

To Be a Woman . . .
Tenderness Personified
Openhearted
Giving Without Measure
Patient Endurance
Tirelessly Serving
Forever Love
Discerning Needs
Arms Outstretched
Remaining Near
Warm Hugs Always Ready
Gentle Caresses
Reassuring Words
Encouraging Smiles
Nurturing Warmth
Loving Even When It Hurts
Listening Ear
Righting Wrongs
Casting out Fear
Strength to the Core
Always Time to Give
Heroic Sacrifices
. . . To Be a Woman!

Sweet Jesus, I love You. Mother Mary, stay with me.

BefrienDing OTHers on THe journey

Ever notice what happens when women get together—even meeting for the first time? Before long, they're swapping stories about birth experiences, children's or grandchildren's antics, and perhaps the latest book they're reading. Many women can make friends with complete strangers just about anywhere! I have made many a friend in a grocery store or on an airplane, among other places. And I'm not talking about a friend for just that moment; I mean a friend who will stay connected.

I met Ellen in a grocery store a few years ago. We continue to discuss our faith, pray for one another, and get together whenever we can. We could have walked right by each other that day. But I thank God that I felt inspired to strike up a conversation with Ellen. If I had walked on by, we would be missing out on the blessings we share. I share the details of meeting Ellen in my book *Feeding Your Family's Soul*.[4]

Amazing things happen when we strive to love with Christ's love, when we ask Him to live and love through us. Women have a gift for befriending others in all sorts of situations. Let's ask Our Lord to use us each day to make friends, keep company, and share our faith with those He puts in our midst. He will use us if we allow Him. Let's push a bit beyond our comfort zones. God will work the miracles!

* *

Joy, to be fruitful, has to be shared.
— St. Teresa of Calcutta

* *

Slow Me Down, Lord

Dear Jesus, open my heart to those around me—those You have chosen to put near me. Please slow my pace and gather my full attention at the times You need me to speak up, reach out, extend my hand, offer a smile, or take the time to listen to one who is craving some love. Help me to see that You are counting on me to use the gifts You have given me to spread Your love and bring others to You. Thank You, Lord, for Your incredible love for me! I love You, Jesus! Amen.

Dear Mother Mary, you went in haste to help your cousin Elizabeth. No doubt you assisted many other women as well. Teach me to be a holy friend to all in need. Please intercede for me so that I will be open to God's promptings in my soul. Amen.

A Reflection on the Joys of Being a Woman

Take some time to reflect upon the joys of your vocation as a woman. What are some ways that you can share the deep, holy joy that resides in your heart? Take a moment and ask Our Lord to show you how. Ask Him to put others within your reach with whom to share your joy and womanly gifts. Don't be afraid to push beyond your comfort zone and expect miracles to happen!

CHAPTER THREE

Challenges Women Face

[N]ow for a little while you may have to suffer various trials, so that the genuineness of your faith, more precious than gold which though perishable is tested by fire, may redound in praise and glory and honor at the revelation of Jesus Christ.

—1 Peter 1:6b–7

Woven into the tapestry of a woman's life are a variety of challenges. Some women seem to endure more than their share of hardship; however, our dear Lord knows what He is doing in our lives. We must trust Him fully. He knows what we can handle and indeed will offer us ample grace to come through our trials and tribulations, drawing closer to Him because of them. And we can strive to extend our hands and heart to help ease the hardships of other women. Our Lord wants us to use our womanly gifts to ease the suffering of others and for His glory.

FATIGUE AND STRESS

No doubt about it, women are hard workers with big hearts, always adding even more to their already demanding schedules to help alleviate the suffering of others. We can be our own worst enemies, too; not wanting to say no, we crowd our hectic days and find ourselves fatigued. Sure, we need to give and help others without measure—but let's pray to discern when to say yes and when we must politely decline, so that we don't increase our stress and fatigue level to our detriment and our family's. As the saying goes: "If Mama ain't happy, ain't nobody happy!"

St. John of the Cross, no stranger to pain and suffering, said, "The soul of one who loves God always swims in joy, always keeps holiday, and is always in the mood for singing." It's not easy to sing when we are fatigued or stressed, but why not try it? Our Lord will give us the grace. We only need to ask Him. Singing—no matter how imperfectly!— during our crazy busy days will help put us in a better mood and benefit those around us, too.

Immaculate Heart of Mary, I love you!

Help Me to Find Balance, Lord

You have given me the heart of a woman, which wants to stretch beyond measure to ease the pain of others. Remind me, Lord, to fix my eyes on my family first, and fulfill their needs according to Your holy will before I attempt to look elsewhere. Help me to know when to say yes and when to say no so that I don't overcommit and can properly serve You, my family, and others—remembering that "love begins at home," as St. Teresa of Calcutta was famous for saying. Amen.

* *

For thou, O LORD, *art my hope, my trust, O*
LORD, *from my youth.*
—Psalm 71:5

* *

Teach Me to Give Jesus a Gift!

Dear Mother Mary, you toiled away caring for your family and household. In addition, you were subjected to many great challenges, being the Mother of our Savior. You understand the burdens women endure. Please intercede for me now because I am weary from the duties of my life and the contradictions from my culture. I will surrender my stress and fatigue over to you rather than gripe and complain, and I hope that by your grace, you will convert my suffering into something more worthy to offer to your Glorious Son. Amen.

Please give me strength, grace, and a hopeful heart, Lord. Amen.

COMPLICATED PREGNANCIES

The gift of life within us is amazingly incredible, something for which we can hardly be thankful enough to God. Along with the joys of our pregnancies, though, come difficulties. God gives prayerful women the grace to endure the suffering to bring new life into the world, but some pregnancies are far more complicated and require close supervision, medical intervention, or bed rest. Let's pray for the unborn all over this world, especially those in danger of abortion. Let's also pray for all the heroic mothers—each one who suffers to bring life into the world, by God's grace.

* *

Peace I leave with you; my peace I give to you; not as the world gives do I give to you. Let not your hearts be troubled, neither let them be afraid.

— John 14:27

* *

Grant My Child Life, Lord

Dear Jesus, help me with my pregnancy, nourish my unborn child, and please grant me all the graces I need at this time. If it is God's holy will, please grant me a safe delivery and a healthy baby. Thank You for Your love for us both. Amen.

* *

Do not be afraid—you are precious to Jesus. He loves you.

—St. Teresa of Calcutta

* *

INFERTILITY

Infertility is a heavy cross that can only truly be understood by those who live with this condition. Let us pray for a deeper understanding of the plight of the infertile so that we may be more caring regarding their quiet, deep suffering, and let us ask Our Lord to unite orphans with deserving hopeful parents through adoption.

Bless These Couples, Lord

Please, Lord, open our hearts to the plight of infertile couples whose arms ache to hold and love a child that they long to raise in their Christian home. Please bless these couples with children to fill their homes with laughter, joy, and so much love. Amen.

Our Lady of Guadalupe, please intercede for me and my spouse as we suffer with infertility. Kindly beseech your Son to grant us the gift of a family, if it be God's holy will for us. Amen.

DIVORCE

Divorce not only severs a marriage in two but also can damage children and families. Sometimes, as dreadful as a divorce is, it's the only means of keeping a family safe and sane, due to serious problems with one spouse or both of them. We, of course, should never judge a divorced person; everyone involved may suffer, and everyone may need to find a way to allow forgiveness to enter their changed lives so that they may recover.

When Catholics divorce, they must be granted an annulment to be allowed by the Church to enter into another marriage. The annulment process can be very healing, helping them move past the pain of divorce and sort out some problems, too. There should be plenty of time to allow for healing and growth before entertaining the thought of entering into another relationship.

Post-divorce is a time to learn more about oneself, and to pray, forgive, heal, and assist the children with their adjustments, too.

Dear Mother Mary, help me to heal from my divorce and to forgive my ex-husband—and myself as well.

* *

Put on then, as God's chosen ones, holy and beloved, compassion, kindness, lowliness, meekness, and patience, forbearing one another and, if one has a complaint against another, forgiving each other; as the Lord has forgiven you, so you also must forgive.
—Colossians 3:12-13

* *

Protect Families from Temptations

Dear Lord, assist me to encourage couples to be strong in their commitment to each other in a world that seems to rip the family apart. Temptations to abandon the family are everywhere, particularly because of modern technology. Help the family to take the time to pray together and keep the allurements of the world at bay. Help couples to realize that real love is a commitment and is sacrificial, not a mere feeling. Please protect families from the snares of the devil. Amen.

St. Michael the Archangel, please protect my family and all families. Amen.

menopause

Menopause is a time that many women secretly dread. It may feel like an unmistakable indication of old age, or feel as if the changes in a woman's body make her somehow less of a woman. But really, it is a brand-new chapter in her journey.

Women at menopause welcome a newfound freedom. Some women can't wait for the change, when they're finally finished with painful menstrual cramps and bloating— although other challenges may present themselves in the form of hot flashes, sometimes sleepless nights, and mood swings. But remember—this too shall pass! And this time can bring added blessings, such as grandchildren!

I love You, Jesus. Please continue to bless me as I journey through this stage of my life. Amen.

• •

Behold, God is my helper; the Lord is the upholder of my life.
—Psalm 54:4

• •

TIME TO PAUSE AND NURTURE

St. Thomas Aquinas said, "Sorrow can be alleviated by good sleep, a bath, and a glass of wine." This sounds good to me! Substitute the words "the discomfort of menopause" for Aquinas's word "sorrow." Let's find moments in our overly packed, hectic lives to give ourselves the pleasure of a hot bath—at least once in a while—or relaxing with a nice glass of wine, hopefully shared with a loved one. Everyone needs a good night's sleep, especially a busy, tired, or challenged woman.

Dear Mother Mary, please help me to ease into and through menopause and accept my new chapter of life. Amen.

sorrows

The loss of a child or spouse is indeed an intense suffering, incredibly difficult to recover from. It may never seem fair when a loved one is snatched away, sometimes abruptly. The intense pain may linger within one's heart, resurfacing at the most unexpected times. However, the beautiful and fond memory of a loved one can live forever in our mind and heart. We must trust the good God that He knows what He is doing. We can surely keep our loved one's soul in prayer and even ask for their intercession for us as we continue on our journey to reach heaven, to be reunited with them one day.

Dear Jesus, help ease my sorrowful heart. Bring me Your peace to soothe my heart and soul. Amen.

* *

Truly, truly, I say to you, you will weep and lament, but the world will rejoice; you will be sorrowful, but your sorrow will turn into joy.
—John 16:20

* *

Mother Mary, Our Lady of Dolors, your heart was pierced with sorrow as the Mother of Jesus; please intercede for me and all the brokenhearted who have suffered the loss of a child or spouse. Please ask the Holy Trinity to grant us the graces we all need. Amen.

Miscarriage

Losing one's baby—once warm and cradled in the womb—to miscarriage is a terrible suffering. I have suffered three miscarriages; in one, I barely escaped death due to severe hemorrhaging. We must trust God that our precious, innocent babies surely go straight into the arms of Jesus and His Mother, Mary. Healing takes time. Be good to yourself. Recognize that miscarriage at any stage is a loss of human life, and the parents need a time of mourning. Offer your sympathies to parents who have miscarried with a warm hug, an offer of prayers, and a listening ear. Most of the time, words are not necessary; rather, the warm gesture of love and compassion is comforting.

Abortion

We know abortion is never acceptable because it is the taking of an innocent human life. However, we need to pray for the countless mothers who have committed this act and who now suffer greatly because of the decision they may have made under duress or in confusion. May they find forgiveness, and may God show His mercy to them and grant them peace.

. . . .

He heals the brokenhearted, and binds up their wounds.
—Psalm 147:3

. . . .

Resting in Your Love and Peace

Dear Jesus, please allow me to lay my face against Your Sacred Heart and rest in Your love, healing, and peace. Amen.

. . . .

Trust in the good God, who loves us, who cares for us, who sees all, knows all, can do all things for my good and the good of souls.
—St. Teresa of Calcutta

. . . .

ESTRANGEMENTS AMONG RELATIVES

Sadly, estrangement among family members is not rare; situations where family members don't speak to one another or have trouble living together come up often in conversation. A woman asked me what she should do about the fact that she can hardly carry on a conversation with her adult daughter because her daughter is often very negative. I advised that she try to uplift her daughter with compliments whenever she can and to remind her daughter of her inner beauty, and that with prayer and love, slowly but surely, their relationship will begin to heal. We must love our family members and pray for them always, and our good Lord will work things out. Of course, no one deserves ill treatment, and if this is the case, it should be addressed and not tolerated. Still, love and prayer are powerful. We need to be patient, hopeful, and loving.

* *

But I call upon God, and the LORD will save me. Evening and morning and at noon I utter my complaint and moan, and he will hear my voice.
—Psalm 55:16–17

* *

My Lord and my God.

* *

Do not be afraid of loving to the point of sacrifice, until it hurts. Jesus' love for us led him to his death.
— St. Teresa of Calcutta

* *

Teach Them to Love and Forgive, Lord

O Lord Jesus, please look kindly upon families everywhere who suffer from painful disagreements and who may hold grudges against one another. Teach them to love and forgive, dear Lord. Amen.

Mother Mary, please intercede for all families and show us how to love. Amen.

THE CULTURE

Women have been exploited and discriminated against throughout history, and the lies and confusion continue today through a culture that demands women become more like men to get ahead and be recognized by peers and society. This can cause a woman to deny her beautiful, unique femininity. When women are striving to become more masculine, pushing their feminine God-given gifts aside, the world becomes lopsided. We need both men and women in our world to complement each other.

Additionally, women face incredible challenges deciphering the mixed messages aimed at them. Under incessant demands for perfection, women may end up depressed. They may worry about everything from "keeping their looks" to proving their worth. They may climb the corporate ladder to the point of exhaustion, sit on countless committees, and wear themselves out on the home front, yet never experience peace or reach their desired "perfection." Let us pray for girls and women all over our world.

· ·

Man, who is the only creature on earth that God willed for its own sake,
cannot fully find himself except through a sincere gift of self.
—*Gaudium et Spes,* 24

· ·

These are beautiful words for us women to ponder in our hearts.

· ·

Let us fall into the hands of the Lord, but not into the hands of men;
for as his majesty is, so also is his mercy.
—Sirach 2:18

· ·

Bless Us with Undeniable Awareness!

O Lord, please weed out our doubts and worries, and bless us women with an undeniable awareness of our God-given gifts and beautiful dignity in Your eyes, so that we may be positively grounded in this awareness and radiate it out to all we meet, helping to alleviate our confusion about our sublime role as women—serving as shining examples to all, leading them to You. Amen.

LEAVING THE NEST

When kids leave the nest, it's only natural to feel bittersweet emotion. When tempted to wallow in sadness over our family's changes, perhaps we can meditate on a passage such as this:

> Do not give yourself over to sorrow, and do not afflict yourself deliberately. Gladness of heart is the life of man, and the rejoicing of a man is length of days. Delight your soul and comfort your heart, and remove sorrow far from you, for sorrow has destroyed many, and there is no profit in it. (*Sirach* 30:21–23)

On one hand, we are sad to see them leave; on the other, we want them to spread their wings and soar! God has big plans for them, and we must release them and trust God. After all, they've only been "on loan" to us so we can help shape them for their journeys ahead. Still, seeing that empty chair at the dinner table pulls so hard on a mother's heart. Of course, we never stop praying for our children and caring for them in other ways, too. I'll let you in on a secret from a mom who has had several children leave the nest already: don't worry, they'll be back! I relish the times my older ones are home for the weekend, a holiday, or even a short visit. We cook a meal together, laugh, reminisce, pray, walk, watch a movie, or play a game. I make sure I snap photos and get in as many hugs and kisses as possible!

Dear Lord, thank You for allowing me the beautiful blessing of raising children and helping to mold their consciences. Please give me the grace, strength, and peace to release them when the time is right. Please surround them with angels and protect them from the snares of the devil, so that they will remain on the road that leads to life! Amen.

Prayer to St. Monica

Dear St. Monica, your powerful motherly prayers saved your wayward son Augustine's soul by God's grace. Please intercede for me and my children who have left the nest to make their way on their own. Please remind me that a mother's prayers are very powerful and that I should never give up hope or ever stop praying for my children's eternal life, no matter where they may wander. Amen.

Mother Mary, help me! Amen.

A Reflection on Women's Challenges

Reflect on the challenges in your life. How can they be used for good? Are you willing to accept what God gives you and offer it back to Him in prayer, asking Him to sanctify it all and bless your life intensely according to His holy will?

Can you offer your pain and suffering for those in danger of losing their souls? How can you help others who are struggling?

Our Lady of Fatima requested that the three young shepherd children offer their sufferings and extra sacrifices for the conversion of sinners. We can do that, too. Pray and look into the eyes of your family members, where Our Lord asks you to start first; then, when all are satisfied at home, Our Lord will surely open the opportunities to show His love elsewhere, too.

CHAPTER FOUR

The Prayers of a Woman

Christ speaks to women about the things of
God, and they understand them; there is a true
resonance of mind and heart, a response of faith.

—St. John Paul II, *Mulieris Dignitatem*

There's no doubt that women's prayers are powerful, but sometimes we need gentle reminders. I believe that Our Lord has given women our many nurturing gifts and loving hearts so that we can pray for all in need. It may be tempting at times to put on blinders and retreat into our own lives, but Our Lord calls us forth to be vessels of healing and inspiration to others.

MeeTing Jesus aT THe WeLL

In John 4:1–30, Jesus is at Jacob's well to offer the Living Water to a Samaritan woman who is there to fetch water for her family. The Samaritan woman realizes who this man is and finally asks for the Living Water. She in turn becomes a missionary, bringing the Word from Jesus to her people, who are then converted. This Gospel story shows us the mystery of prayer.

St. Augustine tells us that Jesus comes to meet every human being as we are "fetching our water." Jesus seeks us first, he explains, asking for a drink, thus expressing His thirst for our love. Jesus's desire for our love "arises from the depths of God's desire for us." How amazing that Our Lord comes to seek us as we are busy "fetching"; how comforting to know that Our Lord comes to find us right where we are, immersed in our work or rest. He loves us that much!

"What no eye has seen, nor ear heard, nor the heart of man conceived, what God has prepared for those who love him," God has revealed to us through the Spirit.
—1 Corinthians 2:9–10a

Thank You, dear Lord, for seeking me out and entering into a dialogue with me. Teach me to seek You out in prayer as often as possible and draw me ever closer still, sweet Jesus! Amen.

THIrSTING FOr THE LIVING WaTEr

In every Missionary of Charity convent around the world, Mother Teresa had two simple, poignant words painted on the wall beside the tabernacle: "I THIRST." The message represents Jesus's thirst for our love and call to us to thirst for His.

"I thirst" is something much deeper than just Jesus saying, "I love you." Until you know deep inside that Jesus thirsts for you, you can't begin to know who He wants to be for you. Or who He wants you to be for Him.
—St. Teresa of Calcutta

Mother Mary, Lead Me

Mother Mary, please lead me to the "well" to have my thirst satiated by your Son, Jesus, and my soul transformed into a vessel to be filled with His Living Water. Help me to be like the Samaritan woman, bringing the Living Water to all I meet, starting first with my family. Amen.

St. Augustine says, "Prayer is the encounter of God's thirst with ours. God thirsts that we may thirst for Him." This profound insight gives us a new way to view prayer—God thirsts for us and wants us to thirst for Him! Our Lord invites us to visit Him at the "well" often.

The Well of Prayer

Dear Jesus, please remind me to visit You often at the "well" where You reside in the Blessed Sacrament; at the "well" at Holy Mass; at the "well" of the Sacrament of Confession; at and the "well" in the center of my life, where I work in my home or workplace, where You are waiting for me to converse with You. Thank You, dear Lord, for Your love. I trust in You! Amen.

Reaching For Jesus's Cloak

* *

And there was a woman who had had a flow of blood for twelve years, and who had suffered much under many physicians, and had spent all that she had, and was no better but rather grew worse. She had heard the reports about Jesus, and came up behind him in the crowd and touched his garment. For she said, "If I touch even his garments, I shall be made well." And immediately the hemorrhage ceased; and she felt in her body that she was healed of her disease.

—Mark 5:25–29

• •

It took faith and courage for the hemorrhaging woman in Mark 5 to make her way through the thick crowd of people surrounding Jesus and reach out and touch His cloak in hope of a cure. In the same way, we women often must brave the crowds of people who may contradict our beliefs to reach out in faith to the One who will heal us. We need to lead countercultural lives of faith and be a holy example to others.

TRUST, FAITH, AND HOPE!

• •

Daughter, your faith has made you well; go in peace, and be healed of your disease.

—Mark 5:34

• •

Jesus responded to the woman who approached Him, whose heart was overflowing with faith, trust, and a whole lot of hope.

Dear Blessed Mother, guide me through the "crowds" to find your Son, so that I can reach out my hand and touch His cloak in prayer. Amen.

At times, we may be hesitant, timid, doubtful, or even fearful; maybe we can't seem to find our way to Jesus's cloak. Perhaps we lack hope. The media and culture target us with all kinds of demands and expectations. Let's hand over all that madness to Our Lord and ask Him to give us peace and an increase in faith, hope, and love. He'll show us the way to His cloak.

Seek some quiet time of Adoration of Jesus in the Blessed Sacrament in which to surrender your heart to Him.

HOLY MOTHER CHURCH GUIDES US

Women were close to Jesus; women learned from Jesus, accepted His teaching, and followed Him. We might want to consider how we can reach out and touch Our Lord's cloak in faith and complete surrender to His will. We live in a different era, no doubt, but we have the benefit of our Holy

Mother Church to teach us and lead us to Jesus. We may be more privileged than the woman who reached out and touched her Savior's cloak, seeking a miracle. Yes, she knew Jesus was a miracle worker, and she was in His presence. But we have the benefit of over two thousand years of Church teaching to help us seek Him.

WAITING PATIENTLY

When it comes to our hope for answers, relief of suffering, or a solution to the myriad difficulties we face, Archbishop Fulton Sheen reminds us:

> There are not two kinds of answers to prayer, but three: One is "Yes." Another is "No." The third is "Wait."

The virtue of patience is a valuable and beneficial gift to pray for.

UNANSWERED PRAYER

Many prayers seem to go unanswered, but Our Lord answers every prayer—the answers just may not be what we expect. We must trust that Jesus knows exactly what we need and when. Our desires may be contrary to what is best for our salvation. Sometimes we need to wait, and other times we need to accept. Our Lord will grant us all necessary graces. He didn't promise us perfect happiness on earth, but rather in the hereafter. Much of our life consists in carrying our crosses, and this, when done lovingly and prayerfully, will win us eternal happiness. Let's beseech Our Lord for a deeper trust in Him.

During our journey through life, Our Lord allows us to rub elbows with those who are without faith so that we can be an example of faith, hope, and love to them. He surely places us in circumstances that help our own faith grow, too.

* *

Patient endurance is the perfection of charity.
—St. Ambrose

* *

No Interrupted Prayers

Dear Jesus, help me truly to understand that in my prayerful role as a woman, I should always strive to fit in as much prayer time as possible. Help me to remember, though, that when my scheduled times of prayer are interrupted, You are not disappointed in me, because my life suddenly becomes transformed into a "prayer" of loving service to those who have "interrupted" my prayer.

WOMEN'S PRAYERS ARE POWERFUL

Mother Mary, let me never forget the power in a woman's prayer! Intercede for me, please, dear Mary. Remind me to pray often so that, by God's grace, I may be an example to all around me, bringing them closer to your Son. Pray with me, dear Mother. Amen.

You only need to reflect upon the prayers of the many women saints throughout history, and your own mother's and grandmothers' prayers, to recognize the immense power in a womans' prayer.

· ·

*Let us love to pray, often feel the need for prayer,
take trouble to pray, for praying enlarges the heart until it is
capable of containing God's gift of Himself.*
—St. Teresa of Calcutta

· ·

Let's begin each day in prayer, offering everything to Our Lord in our own words, or more formally, in the words of the Morning Offering. Then we know that we have given Our Lord everything—full surrender—and that He will take care of every detail throughout our busy day. Let's find every moment that we can offer our heart to Him during the day, keeping a loving conversation going. Our life will then become a prayer.

Morning Offering

O Jesus, through the Immaculate Heart of Mary, I offer You my prayers, works, joys, and sufferings of this day, for all the intentions of your Sacred Heart, in union with the Holy Sacrifice of the Mass throughout the world, in reparation for my sins, for the intentions of all my relatives and friends, and in particular for the intentions of the Holy Father. Amen.

PRAYERS OF GROANING AND SIGHS

Sometimes, we may be so inundated with personal suffering, a heavy heart for others, or just plain busyness, that we are at a loss for how to express ourselves in prayer to Our Lord. At these times, our innermost "groaning" of spirit and the Holy Spirit praying through us combine to become a beautiful prayer, perfect for our present needs.

• •

Likewise, the Spirit helps us in our weakness; for we do not know how to pray as we ought, but the Spirit himself intercedes for us with sighs too deep for words. And he who searches the hearts of men knows what is the mind of the Spirit, because the Spirit intercedes for the saints according to the will of God.

—Romans 8:26–27

• •

A Reflection on the Prayers of a Woman

My prayers with the Lord are my personal loving conversation with Him. I can express myself fully to Him. When I neglect to begin my conversation with Jesus, He comes to meet me wherever I am immersed in the busyness of my life, right where I am "fetching my water." I should look for Him and expect Him. When I am praying, I am encountering Our Lord's presence in His thirst for me and mine for Him. My prayers are powerful and critically important, for my own soul and the souls of all whom I spiritually mother.

CHAPTER FIVE

The Mission of Women

My soul magnifies the Lord, and my spirit
rejoices in God my Savior.

—Luke 1:46b–47

God gives women an important mission: We are expected to accomplish something amazing, by God's grace. That *something* is between God and us. He has a plan, and we should pray for the graces to do Our Lord's holy will. We may lose sight of the "big picture" when we're caught up in the practicalities of our busy daily life. But, as insignificant or small as our daily routines may seem, we shouldn't forget that Our Lord calls women to make a huge difference in our world. This *huge difference* can certainly happen one soul at a time, in the case of a faithful mother who is raising her little saints at home or in encounters with complete strangers when out and about in the community. This can happen one prayer at a time, voiced from a consecrated woman's heart. It also happens on a larger scale when, for example, a Catholic school or hospital is built or a religious order is founded. But, large or small, every task we do in serving others can be transformed into something amazing and beautiful by God's grace and our willingness to offer it to Him with love. Every single little act of love is huge in God's eyes. He will do the work, but He wants to use our loving hands and hearts to reach others.

* *

You must open the interior eyes of your soul on this light, on this heaven within you, a vast horizon stretching far beyond the realm of human activity.

—St. Vincent Ferrer

* *

Awareness of a Mission

Jesus was always aware of being the Servant of the Lord and referred to Himself as a servant, especially when He said, "The Son of man came not to be served but to serve" (Mark 10:45a). The Blessed Mother took her place within her Son's messianic service the moment she conceived Him.

St. John Paul II tells us, "It is precisely this service which constitutes the very foundation of that Kingdom in which to serve means to reign." According to this beloved saint, every person learns "the royal dignity of service" by looking to Christ, the Servant of the Lord. Let us ask ourselves how we are serving Our Lord.

Seeking Humility and a Spirit of Service

Dear Jesus, humble me, so I will understand that my vocation is one of service. You are the Son of the Most High God, and yet You came to serve the world, to serve me. Grant me a spirit of service, and open my heart to put others before myself, striving to serve as You would, dear Lord. Amen.

• •

It is said that humility is truth. The path that will make us more
like Jesus is the path to humility.
—St. Teresa of Calcutta

• •

Am I able to say serenely and in all sincerity, like Our Lady,
"Behold, I am the handmaid of the Lord; let it be to me
according to your word" (*Luke 1:38a*)? Can I offer my life to
God in full surrender? With God's grace, I can!

• •

Oh, virtue of obedience! It can do everything!
—St. Teresa of Ávila

• •

TO SERVE MEANS TO REIGN

It does seem paradoxical, doesn't it?—serving and reigning
at once. But Our Lord Jesus shows us how by the example of
His life and extreme love for mankind. God has also gifted us
with the Blessed Mother whose *fiat* we can pray to emulate,

giving ourselves in service to God to win many souls for the Kingdom of Heaven, remembering that love is not a mere feeling; it is a decision.

. . . .

God seeks us out, one by one. And we ought to answer him, one by one: "Here I am, Lord, because you have called me."
—St. Josemaría Escrivá[5]

. . . .

Prayer to the Holy Spirit

Oh, Holy Spirit, beloved of my soul, I adore You. Enlighten me, guide me, strengthen me, console me. Tell me what I should do; give me Your orders. I promise to submit myself to all that You desire of me and to accept all that You permit to happen to me. Let me only know Your will. Amen.

. . . .

This submission to the Holy Spirit is the Secret of Sanctity.
—Cardinal Mercier

. . . .

CHOOSING

Of course, we have the chance and the right to choose—
God gives us a free will, after all. Even the angels had a
chance to choose to serve God or not, and we know what
happened to Satan, who was once a good angel. Let us be
sure to make the right choices.

* *

Love of obedience is love for the will of God.
—St. Teresa of Calcutta

* *

Humility is a difficult virtue. We want our way and might
have trouble obeying God. But within obedience lies the
secret to true inner peace, joy, and holiness. In order to
obey our state of life, we must pray for humility and live
it well. Being obedient to my state of life means doing all
that is required to fulfill my responsibilities in my vocation
as well as I am able. Many graces are won through humility
and obedience. St. Teresa of Calcutta said, "Fidelity to acts
of obedience becomes like drops of oil that keep the light
of Jesus aflame in our life." What will I choose? Will I be a
luminous flame to light the way for others?

Mother Mary, Help Me

Dear Mother Mary, as pure and as holy as you were, you obeyed God and were humble of heart always. Ask your Son to fill my heart with a humility like His and yours. Amen.

My Distinct Mission

Within all the innumerable things I do as a woman, right down at the core of it all lies the call to my distinct mission from God. I pray that I may fulfill it lovingly throughout each day while praying actively; through my hands, in service; and contemplatively, on my knees—to please God and help my neighbor find his or her way to heaven.

A Reflection on the Mission of Women

God calls you to fulfill a particular mission as a Christian woman. Your mission may not be as obvious as it is to a mother who every day looks into the eyes of her children and is reminded of her role in raising them. You will discover your God-given mission as you prayerfully open your heart and seek to hear Our Lord speak to you. Trust Him with the full surrender of your life.

CHAPTER SIX

Women Are Entrusted

A woman is strong because of her awareness
of this entrusting, strong because of the fact
that God "entrusts the human being to her,"
always and in every way, even in situations
of social discrimination in which she may
find herself.

—St. John Paul II, *Mulieris Dignitatem*

THE HUMAN BEING IS ENTRUSTED TO WOMEN

What a privilege we have as women, being entrusted with the human being! St. John Paul II told us:

> The moral force of a woman is joined to her awareness that God entrusts the human being to her in a special way. Of course, God entrusts every human being to each and every other human being. But this entrusting concerns women in a special way—precisely by reason of their femininity—and this in a particular way determines their vocation. (*Mulieris Dignitatem*)

These are words to ponder in our womanly hearts!

Help Me Embrace This Honor Fully

Dear Lord Jesus, increase my understanding of the great honor that God the Father has bestowed upon me as a woman whose job it is to care for the human being. Help me to become more acutely aware of this entrusting with each passing day, so that I may embrace it fully to please God and to minister to all who have been put in my path. May I pass on Your great love to others through Your grace. Amen.

. . . .

Cast yourself into the arms of God and be very sure that if he wants anything of you, He will fit you for the work and give you strength.
—St. Philip Neri

. . . .

Teach Me to Be Generous, Lord

Dearest Lord, teach me to be generous; teach me to serve You as You deserve; to give and not count the cost, to fight and not heed the wounds, to toil and not seek for rest, to labor and not to ask for reward, except that of knowing I am doing Your will.
—St. Ignatius of Loyola

Mother Mary, teach me to become more aware of the beautiful gift I possess as a woman who is entrusted by God with the human being! Amen.

WOMAN'S RESPONSE TO ENTRUSTING

All women are blessed with the gift of spiritual motherhood because we are entrusted with the human being. We respond to this lofty gift by our responses of love to all we meet. We trust that God knows what He's doing, putting us all together in our families, neighborhoods, parishes, communities, and workplaces for a distinct and holy purpose.

A Prayer of St. Thomas Aquinas

Grant me grace,
O merciful God,
to desire ardently all that is pleasing to thee,
to examine it prudently, to acknowledge it truthfully,
and to accomplish it perfectly,
for the praise and glory of thy name.
Amen.

* *

Hope is patience with the lamp lit.
—Tertullian

* *

The same Jesus who transcended the norms of His culture and treated women tenderly and with great respect when He walked the earth is the Jesus who loves women today. We are affirmed in our God-given dignity as women through St. John Paul II's words:

Everything that has been said so far about Christ's attitude to women confirms and clarifies, in the Holy Spirit, the truth about the equality of man and woman. . . . Both of them—the woman as much as the man—are created in the image and likeness of God. Both of them are equally capable of receiving the outpouring of divine truth and love in the Holy Spirit. Both receive his salvific and sanctifying "visits." (*Mulieris Dignitatem*)

Prayer for Friends

Blessed Mother of those whose names you can read in my heart, watch over them with every care. Make their way easy and their labors fruitful. Dry their tears if they weep; sanctify their joys; raise their courage if they weaken; restore their hope if they lose heart, their health if they be ill, truth if they err, and repentance if they fall. Amen.

—An old French prayer

We learn that there's no running from the cross. Jesus has even told us that we must pick up our cross and follow Him. That's the surest way to heaven. Thomas à Kempis said:

If you carry the cross willingly, it will carry and lead you to the desired goal where indeed there shall be no more suffering, but here there shall be. If you carry it unwillingly, you create a burden for yourself and increase the load, though still you have to bear it. If you cast away one cross, you will find another and perhaps a heavier one. (*The Imitation of Christ*, 2:12)

As we strive to be all Our Lord wants us to be for all those in our midst—those who have been entrusted to us—we invariably stumble upon the cross time and time again. Our

Lord offers us the graces we need to carry our crosses with love. Let's ask Him for His graces.

Jesus, please grant me strength and all the grace I need to endure the hardships of life that beset me. Help me to embrace everything with which You bless me, for Your greater glory and the good of my soul, and the souls of those who have been entrusted to my care. Amen.

A REFLECTION ON BEING ENTRUSTED WITH THE HUMAN BEING

Take time to pray and ponder about the people God has placed in your life—those in your family, neighborhood, workplace, circle of friends, and so on. Are you ministering to them in some way? Are you serving them with love? Is the example of your Christian life making a difference in their lives? We may never see the positive outcome of our Christian love and example. Sometimes we plant the seeds that will blossom later. We hope and pray that, with God's grace, we may be a brilliant light to all.

CHAPTER SEVEN

Mary, a Model for Women

Blessed are you among women, and blessed is
the fruit of your womb!

—Luke 1:42b

The Blessed Trinity found favor with a simple, humble, and faithful Jewish girl. God the Father chose Mary to be the Mother of His Son, Jesus, and she was overshadowed by the Holy Spirit. Mary's *fiat*, "Let it be to me according to your word" (Luke 1:38a), made her the perfect model of faith in God for us—and most worthy of our veneration.

If we stand with Our Lady, she will give us her spirit of loving trust, total surrender, and cheerfulness.
—St. Teresa of Calcutta

HUMAN LIKE US

When we think about the Blessed Mother, most often her greatness comes to mind and we may think we have nothing in common with her. We should remember that she was human like us and needed to pray just like we do. She was no stranger to the realities of everyday life—and experienced more than her share of suffering. She will certainly understand our prayers and pleas to her. She was a woman who understands our hearts.

"Behold the handmaid of the Lord." Our Blessed Mother entrusted her entire life and soul to God! Can we do that as daughters of God?

Prayer to St. Bernadette

Dear St. Bernadette, how I would have loved to be with you during your privileged times with the Blessed Mother! Your unwavering faith, trust, and humility are an awesome inspiration for us all. Please pray for me to the Blessed Mother for the graces that I need most. Pray that I can have an increase in faith to do the things that God calls me to do, no matter how contrary they may seem to the world. Remind me to pray for the conversion of sinners, as you were called to do. St. Bernadette, pray for us and for all who invoke your aid. If it is in God's holy will, please grant me (here mention your request). Amen.

—Donna-Marie Cooper O'Boyle[6]

To Jesus, through Mary.

VIRTUES TO EMULATE

The Blessed Mother gives us much to ponder by the example of her life. Her deep faith was indeed at the foundation of her holiness. Mary lived and moved in faith, hope, and love throughout her entire life. We can pray each day for an increase in faith, hope, and love in our own hearts. After answering God with her courageous "yes," Mary's generous heart compelled her to take a journey into the hill country "in haste" to help her cousin Elizabeth, who was much older than Mary and was also expecting a child. Mary put the discomforts of her own pregnancy aside to serve her older cousin—just as we can do as women of faith, striving to serve Our Lord through those He puts in our families, neighborhoods, workplaces, and communities.

Memorare

Remember, O most gracious Virgin Mary, that never was it known that anyone who fled to thy protection, implored thy help, or sought thy intercession was left unaided.

Inspired by this confidence, I fly unto thee, O Virgin of virgins, my mother, to thee do I come, before thee I stand, sinful and sorrowful.

O Mother of the Word Incarnate, despise not my petitions, but in thy mercy hear and answer me. Amen.

* *

Totus Tuus (Totally Yours)
—St. John Paul II, his apostolic motto,
indicating devotion to the Blessed Mother

* *

We can learn much from our Blessed Mother's simplicity, courage, obedience, wisdom, and love. She was mindful that a bride and groom at Cana were without wine at their wedding feast and asked her Son to perform a miracle. "Do whatever he tells you," she instructed the wine stewards, leaving it all in her Son's capable hands.

. . . .

Oh, how I love the Blessed Virgin! She is more a mother than a Queen.
—St. Thérèse of the Child Jesus

. . . .

Mother Mary, Mother Me!

Dear Mary, please help me in my role as a woman who mothers others. Please pray for me to have strength never to shirk my duties, and grant me an extra dose of love to reach out with compassion to all in my care. When I'm tired or in need of comfort, please allow me to rest my head against your sweet Immaculate Heart, dear Mary, safe within the folds of your mantle! Amen.

. . . .

Mary, Mother of Jesus, be Mother to me now!
—taught to the author by St. Teresa of Calcutta

. . . .

Mary's Sorrowful Heart

Facing rejection from dear St. Joseph
and possible death by stoning,
taken away from your home late in pregnancy,
rejected again when searching for a birth place
for the Savior of the world.
A sword of sorrow pierced your heart
when your baby was presented in the Temple.
Later on, frantically searching for your child.
Feeling the sting of rejection when your Son was unwelcomed by others.
Finally, to watch as He suffered Calvary
and a cruel death on the Cross;
He then lay dead in your arms.
Mary, you know.
Pray for me, please.
Amen.

Mary's holy voice caused John the Baptist to leap for joy in St. Elizabeth's womb (Luke 1:44). Luke teaches us that the Blessed Mother is our mighty intercessor. We should call upon her often for her help. She is very powerful over all evil and crushes the head of the serpent.

* *

O Mary, conceived without sin, pray for us who have recourse to thee.
—Miraculous Medal Prayer of St. Catherine Labouré

* *

May Mary, Queen of Love, watch over women and their mission in service of humanity, of peace, of the spread of God's Kingdom!
—St. John Paul II, *Letter to Women*

Mary, Help of Christians, come to my aid. Assist me in my temporal needs, and help me to live in such a manner that I may obtain the promise of everlasting life. Amen.

A REFLECTION ON OUR BLESSED MOTHER

Take some time to reflect upon Mary's place within your life. Do you converse with her? Do you give her the veneration due to her as the Mother of God? Do you fear approaching her? She is ready and waiting to be your Mother.

CHAPTER EIGHT

Feminine Genius

I will give you as a light to the nations,
that my salvation may reach to the
end of the earth.

—Isaiah 49:6c

The term "feminine genius" is attributed to St. John Paul II, but the concept goes back to Pope Pius XII. The Second Vatican Council highlighted the distinctly feminine contributions to society. St. John Paul II's Apostolic Letter *Mulieris Dignitatem* reflected on the spiritual and moral strength of women and gave practical ways to apply our *feminine genius* to the world. Later, his *Letter to Women* addressed challenges to women in our modern times and offered a warning to women to be cautious of destructive feminist ideologies.

* *

In all its expressions, womanhood is part of the essential heritage of mankind and the Church herself.
—St. John Paul II, *Letter to Women*

* *

* *

In fact, woman has a genius all her own, which is vitally essential to both society and the Church.
—St. John Paul II, Angelus address, July 23, 1995

* *

* *

I will, I want, with God's blessing, to be holy.
—St. Teresa of Calcutta

* *

How to Use Our Feminine Gifts

St. John Paul II reminds us in *Mulieris Dignitatem:*

> From the beginning of Christ's mission, women show
> to him and to his mystery a special sensitivity which is
> characteristic of their femininity.

He pointed out that women were not only faithful to Jesus at
the Cross; they were first at His tomb, first to find it empty,
first to hear the message, "He is not here. He has risen, as he
said." They were first to embrace His feet and first to be called
to announce the news to the apostles. Mary Magdalene was
first to meet the risen Christ, bearing witness to the apostles.
St. John Paul II tells us, "This event, in a sense, crowns all
that has been said previously about Christ entrusting divine
truths to women as well as men."

- -

Tell aching mankind to snuggle close to My merciful heart,
and I will fill it with peace.
—Jesus to St. Faustina Kowalska[7]

- -

Can we pass along the message of mercy from Jesus? Yes,
we can!

. . . .

The Church sees in Mary the highest expression of the "feminine genius," and she finds in her a source of constant inspiration. Mary called herself the "handmaid of the Lord" (Lk 1:38). Precisely through this service, Mary was able to experience in her life a mysterious but authentic "reign." It is not by chance that she is invoked as "Queen of heaven and earth." The entire community of believers thus invokes her; many nations and peoples call upon her as their "Queen." For her, "to reign" is to serve! Her service is "to reign"!

—St. John Paul II, *Letter to Women*

. . . .

Lord, Open Our Eyes

Lord, open our eyes, that we may see You in our brothers and sisters. Lord, open our ears, that we may hear the cries of the hungry, the cold, the frightened, the oppressed. Lord, open our hearts, that we may love each other as You love us. Renew in us Your spirit. Lord, free us and make us one.

—St. Teresa of Calcutta

. . . .

The hour is coming, indeed has come, in which the vocation of women is being acknowledged in its fullness; the hour which women acquire in the world an influence, an effect, and a power never hitherto achieved.

That is why at this moment, when the human race is undergoing so

deep a transformation, women, imbued with the spirit of the Gospel,
can do so much to aid mankind in not falling.
—Closing documents of Vatican II

. . . .

These are powerful words upon which women can meditate.

Dear Lord, grant me the wisdom and grace to understand my God-given gifts, my "feminine genius," so that I may use all that I have for Your greater glory and the good of others. Amen.

A LUMINOUS BEACON OF HOPE

Women today must work hard to build a culture of life. Let's be sure to ask our dear Lord to bless us with all we need to carry out His holy will. Try your best to carve out regular times of prayer, not getting discouraged when your prayers are "interrupted" by those who need you, because it is then that your meditative or contemplative prayer becomes an active prayer in the service of others. Make time to visit Jesus in Adoration of the Blessed Sacrament when you can be at His feet to allow Him to speak to your heart. With His grace, we can be a healing balm, a radiant example—a luminous beacon of hope to light the way to heaven for others! Let us never neglect to do our part!

A Reflection on Our Feminine Genius

Women in all their varied roles discover their dignity and worth within their sacrificial giving and service to others. God gives women many beautiful feminine gifts to use for His glory and the good of others. Let's ask Him to help us become more aware of our gifts and be especially attentive to those we should minister to by His grace. Many times, in order to help others, we must push beyond our comfort zones to speak to strangers and share our faith and our hearts. But, I find, those times are precisely when God's transforming miracles happen in human hearts! We are beckoned by Our Lord to pray for others throughout every circumstance—called to use our loving feminine gifts to help those in need, offering precious hope and resplendent inspiration to light the world! Let your light shine, dear sister in Christ!

Lord, live in us and shine through us. Grant us an increased faith in Your everlasting love for us. Amen.

ACKNOWLEDGMENTS

I am most grateful to Jacquelyn Lindsey at Our Sunday Visitor Publishing Company for having faith in me to go forward with the first edition of this book. I owe a debt of gratitude to Robert Edmonson and Phil Fox Rose of Paraclete Press for partnering with me to produce this beautiful second edition. My thanks, as well, to the wonderful team at Paraclete Press for their excellent work. It's been a special blessing to work with them.

As always, I am thankful to my parents and my family: my mother, Alexandra Mary Uzwiak Cooper, and my father, Eugene Joseph Cooper, in loving memory and thanksgiving for bringing me into this world. In loving memory and gratitude to my grandmother Alexandra Theresa Karasiewicz Uzwiak for her inexhaustible love, guidance, and inspiration. Thanks to my godparents, Alfred Uzwiak and Bertha Uzwiak Barosky. Also, my thanks to the blessing of my brothers and sisters: Alice Jean, Gene, Gary, Barbara, Tim, Michael, and David. You are all so dear to my heart.

My children, Justin, Chaldea, Jessica, Joseph, and Mary-Catherine, are my life and vocation. I love you! And to my husband, David, thank you for your continuous loving support. I love you! And my grandson, Shepherd James, I love you, too!

Thank you to dear Mother Teresa for her love and guidance while on earth and now from heaven, and to Fr. John A. Hardon, SJ, my former spiritual director, for his wonderful spiritual direction, which continues from heaven. Thanks to Fr. Andrew Apostoli, CFR, for his friendship, support, and prayers, and for the steadfast caring prayer support from my wonderful "Sisters in Christ"! To my readers, thank you for the gift of your friendship and journeying along with me. Let us together pray to pave the way to heaven for others by God's grace! God love you!

NOTES

1   *Which stands up better in a crisis*   Fulton J. Sheen, *The World's First Love* (New York: McGraw-Hill, 1952), 149.

2   *Letter to Women*   See http://bit.ly/1UaSKxz

3   *Apostolic Letter* Mulieris Dignitatem   See http://bit.ly/2nlN4Ph

4   *Feeding Your Family's Soul*   Donna-Marie Cooper O'Boyle, *Feeding Your Family's Soul: Dinner Table Spirituality* (Brewster, MA: Paraclete Press, 2016), 57–58.

5   *God seeks us out*   Josemaría Escrivá de Balaguer, *Christ Is Passing By: Homilies* (Chicago: Scepter Press, 1974), 174, par. 2.

6   *Dear St. Bernadette*   Donna-Marie Cooper O'Boyle, *Catholic Saints Prayer Book: Moments of Inspiration from Your Favorite Saints* (Huntington, IN: Our Sunday Visitor, 2008), 19.

7   *Tell aching mankind to snuggle close*   St. Maria Faustina Kowalska, *Diary of Saint Maria Faustina Kowalska: Divine Mercy in My Soul* (Stockbridge, MA: Marian Press, 2005), par. 1074.

ABOUT THE AUTHOR

Donna-Marie Cooper O'Boyle, a Catholic wife and mother of five and grandmother, was chosen by the Pontifical Council for the Laity to participate in an International Women's Congress to study *Mulieris Dignitatem: On the Dignity and Vocation of Woman* at the Vatican. She is a speaker, catechist, pilgrimage host, and retreat leader, and was blessed to know St. Teresa of Calcutta for ten years. Donna-Marie's frequent appearances on national radio and television, her books, and her speaking engagements are the public face of a life devoted to seeking holiness in the context of a happy Catholic family. She is the television host of EWTN's *Everyday Blessings for Catholic Moms*, *Catholic Mom's Café*, and *Feeding Your Family's Soul*. She is the best-selling and award-winning author of more than twenty books, including her memoir, *The Kiss of Jesus*, as well as *Mother Teresa and Me: Ten Years of Friendship*, *The Miraculous Medal*, *My Confirmation Book*, *Angels for Kids*, *Feeding Your Family's Soul: Dinner Table Spirituality*, *Our Lady of Fatima: 100 Years of Stories, Prayers, and Devotions*, and *Our Lady's Messages to Three Shepherd Children and the World*.

In addition to her books, Donna-Marie's writing can be found in Catholic magazines, newspapers, online, in her columns, and on her website and blogs. She can be reached through her websites: donnacooperoboyle.com and feedingyourfamilyssoul.com.

ABOUT PARACLETE PRESS

WHO WE ARE

Paraclete Press is a publisher of books, recordings, and DVDs on Christian spirituality. Our publishing represents a full expression of Christian belief and practice—from Catholic to Evangelical, from Protestant to Orthodox.

We are the publishing arm of the Community of Jesus, an ecumenical monastic community in the Benedictine tradition. As such, we are uniquely positioned in the marketplace without connection to a large corporation and with informal relationships to many branches and denominations of faith.

WHAT WE ARE DOING

PARACLETE PRESS BOOKS | Paraclete publishes books that show the richness and depth of what it means to be Christian. Although Benedictine spirituality is at the heart of all that we do, we publish books that reflect the Christian experience across many cultures, time periods, and houses of worship. We publish books that nourish the vibrant life of the church and its people.

We have several different series, including the best-selling Paraclete Essentials and Paraclete Giants series of classic texts in contemporary English; Voices from the Monastery—men and women monastics writing about living a spiritual life today; award-winning poetry; best-selling gift books for children on the occasions of baptism and first communion; and the Active Prayer Series that brings creativity and liveliness to any life of prayer.

MOUNT TABOR BOOKS | Paraclete's newest series, Mount Tabor Books, focuses on the arts and literature as well as liturgical worship and spirituality, and was created in conjunction with the Mount Tabor Ecumenical Centre for Art and Spirituality in Barga, Italy.

PARACLETE RECORDINGS | From Gregorian chant to contemporary American choral works, our recordings celebrate the best of sacred choral music composed through the centuries that create a space for heaven and earth to intersect. Paraclete Recordings is the record label representing the internationally acclaimed choir Gloriæ Dei Cantores, praised for their "rapt and fathomless spiritual intensity" by *American Record Guide;* the Gloriæ Dei Cantores Schola, specializing in the study and performance of Gregorian chant; and the other instrumental artists of the Arts Empowering Life Foundation.

Paraclete Press is also privileged to be the exclusive North American distributor of the recordings of the Monastic Choir of St. Peter's Abbey in Solesmes, France, long considered to be a leading authority on Gregorian chant.

PARACLETE VIDEO | Our DVDs offer spiritual help, healing, and biblical guidance for a broad range of life issues including grief and loss, marriage, forgiveness, facing death, bullying, addictions, Alzheimer's, and spiritual formation.

Learn more about us at our website:
www.paracletepress.com or phone us
toll-free at 1.800.451.5006

SCAN
TO
READ
MORE